DATE DUE
Fecha Para Retornar

Welcome to the Rodeo!

Josepha Sherman

Heinemann Library
Chicago, Illinois

Customer Service 888-454-2279

Designed by Lisa Buckley
Printed in Hong Kong

04 03 02 01 00
10 9 8 7 6 5 4 3 2 1

Library of Congress Cataloging-in-Publication Data
Sherman, Josepha.
    Welcome to the rodeo!/ Josepha Sherman.
        p. cm. – (Rodeo)
    Includes bibliographical references (p.) and index.
    Summary: Introduces the rodeo as a sport, exploring its origins, people, animals, events, scoring, and involvement of children.
        ISBN 1-57572-508-8 (library binding)
        1. Rodeos—Juvenile literature. [1. Rodeos.] I. Title.
    GV1834. S545 2000
    791.8'4—dc21
                                                    99-048966

Acknowledgments
The author and publishers are grateful to the following for permission to reproduce copyright material:
Corbis-Bettmann, p. 4; Corbis-Bettmann/UPI, pp. 5, 22; Dudley Barker, pp. 6, 9; Steve Bly, pp. 7, 8, 10, 23; Erwin C. "Bud" Nielsen/Images International, pp. 11, 16, 24; Jonathon Wright/Photographers/Aspen, p. 12; Ted Streshinsky/Photo 20-20, p. 13; Esbin-Anderson/Photo 20-20, p. 14; Wilbur E. Garrett/National Geographic, p. 15; Valrie Massey/Photo 20-20, p. 17; Dan Hubbell, p. 18 (both); Peter Weimann/Animals Animals, p. 19; Jack Upton, p. 20; The Granger Collection, p. 21; Winfield I. Parks, Jr./National Geographic, p. 25; Randy Olson/National Geographic, p. 26; William A. Allard/National Geographic, p. 27; AP/Wide World, p. 28.

Cover photograph: Bob Daemmrich/Photo

Special thanks to Dan Sullivan of the Calgary Stampede for his comments in the preparation of this book.

Every effort has been made to contact copyright holders of any material reproduced in this book. Any omissions will be rectified in subsequent printings if notice is given to the publisher.

Some words are shown in bold, **like this.**
You can find out what they mean by looking in the glossary.

Contents

Cowboy Fun to Professional Sport

No one knows exactly when the rodeo first began, because many towns claim to have held "The First Rodeo." What we do know is that somewhere in the middle of the 1800s, working cowboys in the United States and Canada began showing off to each other, testing their roping and riding skills. Maybe one cowboy could catch a calf faster than anyone else, while another cowboy could ride even the wildest of horses. Soon the cowboys were holding contests just for fun whenever they got together at **cattle** roundups, cattlemen conventions, and **Wild West Shows**.

The word *rodeo* is a Spanish word that means corral or roundup. This is where **broncos** were trained. As cowboys made their work into contests, the name rodeo also came to mean the game of cowboy skills.

The Rodeo Association of America was founded in 1929. Rodeos became professional contests for prizes and money.

Rodeos are sometimes held in indoor arenas.

Today, rodeos can be found all over the United States and Canada. More than 600 rodeos each year are Professional Rodeo Cowboys Association events. But there are about 8,000 other rodeos held in North America each year. Rodeos might be small events held at state fairs and have small prizes for the winners. Other rodeos can be large professional events, such as the Calgary Stampede in Canada, that last for several days and end with winners receiving money and titles, such as World Champion Cowboy.

Every rodeo rider hopes to earn enough prize money to make a good living. But more than that, every rider dreams of earning a place in rodeo history as a true champion.

What Happens at a Rodeo?

A rodeo is as exciting and colorful as a circus.

A rodeo is a noisy place. **Cattle** bawl from their pens, horses whinny to each other, and people in the grandstands laugh and shout with excitement. It's a cheerful, colorful place where cowboys and cowgirls wear colorful shirts and jeans, and rodeo clowns dress as brightly as ragged rainbows. Maybe the air is a little dusty and smells of horses and cattle, but nobody really minds that.

A Miss Rodeo America Pageant is held every year. The winner may earn thousands of dollars in scholarship money.

There are no rules about how many events must be included in a rodeo, and the rules differ as to who can compete. Larger rodeos usually only allow professional rodeo riders to enter. Smaller rodeos allow beginners to try their luck. There is also a competition for women in which they can show off their riding ability, social grace, and confidence. The winner of that contest will be crowned Miss Rodeo or Rodeo Queen.

But no matter who is competing, all rodeos usually have six major rodeo events. Some events have been invented just for the rodeo show!

Traditional Horseback Events

A cowboy has to stay on the bucking bronc's back for a full eight seconds. That seems like a long time when the horse doesn't want him there!

The horse on a North American ranch in the 1800s was very important. A cowboy on horseback could herd **cattle,** catch calves, and ride long miles to check for gaps in fences. There usually wasn't much time to break, or tame, a wild horse that would buck wildly to get a cowboy off its back. Today, gentler training methods are used, but bucking horse events are still a part of every rodeo.

Saddle Bronc Riding: **Bronc** or **bronco** is a name for a bucking horse. A saddle bronc rider must stay in the saddle for a full eight seconds.

Bareback Bronc Riding: A bareback bronc rider doesn't have a saddle to help him stay on for the full eight seconds. He has only his **rigging.** Rigging is a circle of leather around the middle of the horse. It also has a handle for the cowboy to hold onto with one hand.

Cutting: In this event the rider and the horse work together as a team. The rider directs the horse to keep a cow from rejoining a herd. A good cow horse can make quick turns and jumps.

The rodeo event of cutting comes from ranch work. On the range, cowboys use their horses to separate, or "cut," a cow from the rest of the herd.

Traditional Roping Events

Raising **cattle** has always been the main business of a ranch. In fact, most of the meat in supermarkets today comes from ranch cattle. Tending the cattle has always been the cowboy's major job. On modern ranches, cowboys may ride in a jeep or a helicopter to get to a cattle herd. But once there, the modern cowboy still rides a horse into the herd, just the way it was done more than 150 years ago. Today's cowboy still uses roping skills, too, to **lasso** a calf for branding or to give it medicine.

In the calf roping event, the cowboy has to rope, then tie the calf.

A pair of team roping cowboys prepares to rope a steer.

Calf Roping: In this rodeo event, a cowboy on horseback lassoes a 200- to 300-pound (91–136 kilogram) running calf. The horse keeps the rope tight so the calf cannot escape while the cowboy jumps off his horse, grabs the calf, and throws the calf on its back. If the calf is already down on the ground when the cowboy gets to it, the cowboy must get the calf back on its feet so it can be tossed. Then he ties together any three of the calf's legs using a six-foot (two meter) rope called a **piggin' string**. The calf must stay securely tied for six seconds.

Team Roping: In ranch work, two cowboys work together to rope a **steer** that is too big or bad-tempered to be safely caught by one man. In the rodeo, the goal is for a two-man team on horseback to lasso a running steer. They do this by having one rider rope the horns and the other rider rope the hind legs, as quickly as possible.

Other Cowboy and Cattle Events

A steer can weigh as much as 500 pounds (227 kilograms). A cowboy can have quite a job wrestling it to the ground.

Not every event at a rodeo is based on everyday ranch activities. Cowboys enjoy testing their abilities as much as anyone else, and since **cattle** are part of their working life, they became part of their sports life as well.

Steer Wrestling: This event was invented around 1900 by an African-American cowboy, Bill Pickett, who was born in the late 1800s. It is also called bulldogging, because long ago, a cowboy might bite the **steer's** nose or lip, like a bulldog would, to get the steer under control. This is another event in which the cowboy and the horse work as a team. Leaping from his **galloping** horse, a contestant grabs a running steer by the right horn and wrestles it to the ground. All four of the downed steer's feet have to be pointing in the same direction. The winning cowboy is the one who does this faster than anyone else.

Bull Riding: This is the most dangerous of the rodeo events. The cowboy has nothing to hang onto but the **bull rope**, a flat, braided rope about the bull's body. A 2,000-pound (907 kilogram) bull will do his best to throw off the cowboy. Then the bull might try to trample or gore him. **Rodeo clowns** often risk their lives to draw the bull away from a fallen cowboy.

Alert rodeo clowns watch a bull rider, ready to help if they're needed.

Speed and Agility Events

A horse and rider speed around a barrel.

Cowboys and cowgirls enjoy showing off their agility at high speeds, as well as the ability of their horses.

Barrel Racing: A rider, usually a girl or woman, must race her horse through a **cloverleaf pattern** around three barrels. The horse moves fast with a cat's grace and agility as it turns as close to the barrels as possible without knocking them over or losing speed. Then the cowgirl rides her horse to the finish line as quickly as possible.

Chuck Wagon Racing: This event, known as Rangeland Derby at the big Calgary Stampede in Canada, is wild and dangerous. It is included in only a few rodeos. In ranch work, a chuck wagon holds the food and extra gear for working cowboys. It was never designed to race. However, in the chuck wagon race, each wagon is pulled by four horses, while four cowboys on horseback, called outriders, help guide the team in a figure-eight pattern. Then the chuck wagon teams go full speed on a track, with the outriders trying to stay within 125 feet (38 meters) of the wagon as it **gallops** across the finish line.

A chuck wagon racer has to control four galloping horses and keep the wagon from turning over.

Animal Stars

There could be no rodeo without the animals. **Broncs**, cutting horses, calves, **steers,** and bulls are the real stars of the show.

Nobody in a rodeo wants an animal to be harmed. One reason why the animals are well-treated is because they are expensive. The average bucking horse might sell for $5,000, but a good bucking horse can cost more than $25,000.

There are rules covering the amount of time each animal spends in a rodeo. The average bucking horse works only eight seconds in a rodeo. Even with appearances in many rodeos, a bronco needs to buck only for about five minutes a year.

Animals at rodeos are kept in large pens. Between events, the animals are fed and watered.

A bucking horse may pass her good qualities on to her foal.

There's no retirement age for broncs or bulls. They usually remain in the rodeo circuit as long as they are healthy and willing to buck. Once an animal loses interest, though, it is retired. One bucking bronc named Cindy Rocket was still working rodeos at the age of 29 years. Cindy Rocket lived and performed long beyond the average life of a good trail horse. Calves and steers may be used in rodeos for only one year.

There's an additional benefit to keeping rodeo animals happy and healthy. A retired bull can father calves, and a bucking **mare** can have **foals**. Bucking is a quality that gets passed down from generation to generation. Not all horses or bulls will buck, so retired rodeo animals might produce a new generation of performers.

Safety of the Animals

Some people see a cowboy's spurs or the **flank straps** that **broncos** wear and think that rodeo animals are being mistreated or put into danger. This isn't true. Any cowboy found with sharpened spurs is banned from competition. The flank strap, which goes around a horse's middle, is fleece-lined. A 160-pound (73 kilogram) man could not fasten it tight enough to hurt a 1,200-pound (544 kilogram) animal. As the horse tries to flick off the strap, it bucks. Even a **foal** will buck if someone touches it on the flank.

Rodeo animals are injured less often than animals who live on the open range. Each year ranchers lose many animals from their herds due to severe weather, predators, broken legs from stepping into holes, and man-made obstacles, such as barbed wire fences. None of these dangers are present in the rodeo environment.

The rowels on a rodeo rider's spurs are blunted, so that they cannot hurt the animal.

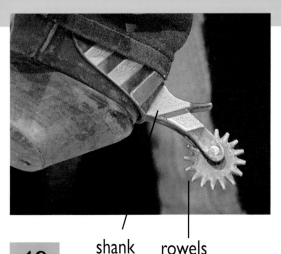

shank   rowels

blunt rowels

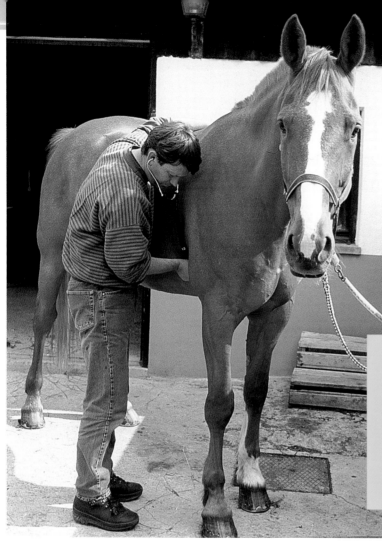

Trained workers take good care of the rodeo animals and make sure they stay healthy.

Surveys show that only one rodeo animal out of two thousand has any sort of injury in a year. One reason for the low rate of injuries are the rules every rodeo must follow.

✪ Every animal must be inspected by a veterinarian before a rodeo event. A hurt or sick animal is withdrawn from competition.

✪ Every animal must be properly fed and watered before, during, and after a rodeo.

✪ Anyone found deliberately hurting a rodeo animal must be fined and may be banned from all rodeos.

Cowboys

Anyone can enter an amateur rodeo, but a cowboy has to win a certain number of events in smaller rodeos before he can enter a professional rodeo. There he competes against cowboys with more experience. If he can win in these rodeos, a cowboy can call himself a professional.

In the early days of rodeos, cowboys usually came from ranches. Many rodeo cowboys do not work on ranches today. They follow the rodeo circuit. A rodeo cowboy doesn't earn a salary. He relies on prize money to pay for his entrance fees, travel, and living expenses.

Most professional cowboys make less than $50,000 a year going from rodeo to rodeo.

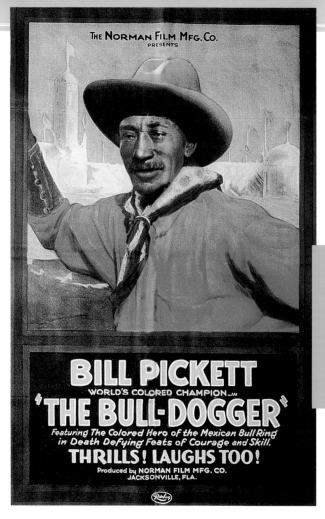

THE NORMAN FILM MFG. CO.
PRESENTS

BILL PICKETT
WORLD'S COLORED CHAMPION IN
'THE BULL-DOGGER'
Featuring The Colored Hero of the Mexican Bull Ring
in Death Defying Feats of Courage and Skill.
THRILLS! LAUGHS TOO!
Produced by NORMAN FILM MFG. CO.
JACKSONVILLE, FLA.

This poster advertises the African-American cowboy who invented the sport of **steer** wrestling or "bulldogging."

African-American cowboys have always been part of the ranch and rodeo worlds. Today, African-American cowboys perform in all the big rodeos. Touring events, such as the Bill Pickett Invitational Rodeo, bring the rodeo to Los Angeles, Alabama, and Washington, DC.

Native Americans also took part in early ranch and rodeo activities. Today they participate in the national rodeos and in Native American sponsored events, such as the Indian National Finals Rodeo held yearly in Albuquerque, New Mexico.

Today, rodeo competitors in North America also come from Australia, New Zealand, Brazil, Mexico, Germany, Japan, and Italy.

Cowgirls

This 1936 Rodeo Queen was chosen because she could rope and ride wild horses.

In the 1800s, ranch women grew up having the same skills as ranch men. In fact, since qualified hands, or workers, were often scarce, women sometimes did the same work as men. They could tame horses and rope and brand **cattle.** In the early days of rodeo and into the twentieth century, cowgirls performed in the same events as the cowboys, riding **broncs** and roping calves. There were even some women bull riders.

But rodeo committees grew nervous about letting women perform in such a dangerous sport as rodeo, even if the cowgirls themselves weren't worried. There might even have been some envy on the part of the cowboys, because cowgirls sometimes won against them.

In 1930, the rodeo committees banned cowgirls from all rodeo events, except for the relatively safe sport of barrel racing and the Miss Rodeo contests. Many of these rules have since been relaxed, but most female contestants are still barrel racers.

Not all modern cowgirls are happy with the restrictions. The barrel racers challenged the rodeo committees, and in 1996, the Calgary Stampede rodeo made barrel racing an equal major event. Other rodeo committees followed in 1998. Thanks to that victory, the money and prizes awarded to barrel racers are now equal to those awarded in the traditional men's events.

Most barrel racers are girls or women.

23

People Who Make the Rodeo Possible

Rodeo clowns distract a bull to keep a rider from getting hurt.

It isn't just cowboys and cowgirls who make a rodeo possible. It takes many people to put on the show.

Rodeo clowns: Their main job at a rodeo is to protect the bull riders. When they aren't working to keep a fallen cowboy from getting trampled, they entertain the audience. In the middle of all the wild excitement of a rodeo, a little humor can be welcome!

Pickup riders: These people on horseback aren't contestants, but they are very necessary. A pickup rider picks up bareback and saddle **bronc** riders from a moving bronco when the cowboy's ride is done. Then he leads the horse from the arena.

Stock contractor: The stock contractor provides healthy horses, calves, **steers,** and bulls to local rodeo committees. The contractors own the animals and the trucks and trailers used to transport them from show to show. The contractor might even provide the rodeo announcer and the entertainment, too.

The judges: These men and woman are the officials who keep the score for the rodeo events and make sure that all the rules are obeyed.

The announcer: This person introduces the events and each contestant and announces the names of each horse and bull.

The rodeo secretary: He or she keeps track of all the entries, the fees paid, the order of contestants, the scores, and the event records. The secretary also makes sure that the winners get their prizes.

A pickup rider helps a bareback rider off his horse.

From Kids to Professionals

Children who grow up on ranches or in areas where rodeos are held may want to take part in the events. And they can, because rodeos often include special events for children.

Very young children, those under five years old, can try roping a dummy **steer.** This is sometimes a bale of hay with a plastic steer-shaped head. Boys and girls a few years older try to rope a live calf that is standing still. It's not until much later that they can try roping a moving calf from a moving horse.

This cowboy will have to practice more before he can rope both horns of the dummy.

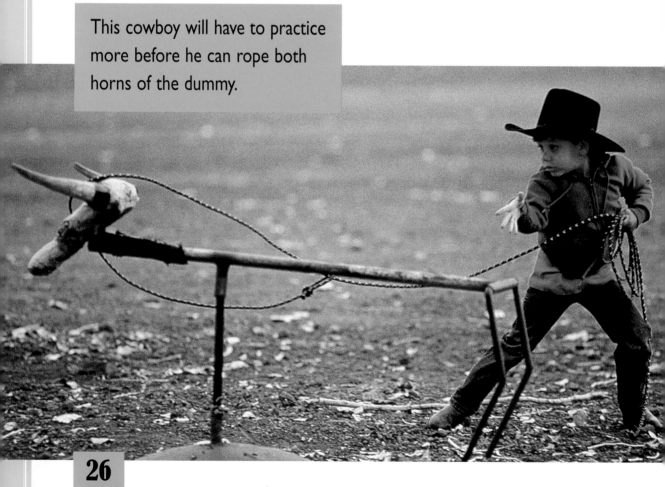

A **rodeo clown** runs to help a calf rider after the ride.

The bull riding event for very young children certainly doesn't begin with a bull. Very young children first ride a sheep. Then, when they are six years old, they might try the calf riding competition. Older boys, from about eight to fourteen, can graduate to steer riding, since a steer is bigger than a calf but gentler than a bull. Some boys may even be riding the gentler bulls by age fourteen. By their late teens, boys can enter all the adult rodeo events.

The only event that doesn't have any age requirement is barrel racing. Girls can enter barrel racing competitions as soon as they can ride well enough. The youngest barrel racer was only five years old. Children may actually be professional barrel racers before they're fifteen.

Rodeo Today

Today, most rodeos are still found in the Western United States and Canada. There are permanent yearly events like the Calgary Stampede, held in Calgary, Canada, and smaller rodeos that are held all over North America, from California to Pennsylvania. Traveling rodeos bring the sport to cities as far east as New York City and Boston. And rodeos can even be found in other countries, such as Australia and Japan.

Steer wrestling is an event that is found at rodeos everywhere.

Museums and Associations

Museums:

Amon Carter Museum
3501 Camp Bowie Boulevard
Fort Worth, Tex. 76107
(817) 738-1933
Fax (817) 377-8523

Autry Museum
   of Western Heritage
4700 Western Heritage Way
Los Angeles, Calif. 90027
(323) 667-2000

National Cowboy Hall of Fame
1700 NE 63rd Street
Oklahoma City, Okla. 73111
(405) 478-2250

National Cowgirl Museum
   and Hall of Fame
111 West 4th Street
Fort Worth, Tex. 76102
(817) 336-4475
Fax (817) 336-2470

The Pro Rodeo Hall of Fame
   and Museum of the
   American Cowboy
Exit 147 – I-25
Colorado Springs, Colo. 80919
(719) 528-4764

Associations:

American Junior Rodeo Association
6029 Loop 306 South
San Antonio, Tex. 76905
(915) 651-2572
Fax: (915) 651-2572

Canadian Professional Rodeo
   Association
#223, 2116 27th Avenue, NE
Calgary, AB, Canada T2E 7A6
(403) 250-7440

National High School Rodeo
   Association
11178 North Huron, Suite #7
Denver, Colo. 80234
(303) 452-0820
Fax (303) 452-0912

National Little Britches Rodeo
   Association
1045 West Rio Grande
Colorado Springs, Colo. 80906
(719) 389-0333

Professional Rodeo Cowboys
   Association
101 Pro Rodeo Drive
Colorado Springs, Colo. 80919
(800) 763-3648

Women's Professional Rodeo
   Association
235 Lake Plaza Drive, Suite 134
Colorado Springs, Colo. 80906
(719) 576-0900

Professional Rodeo World Records

Youngest World Champion

Jim Rodriguez, Jr., age 18   1959 Team Roping

Oldest World Champion

Ike Rude, age 59   1953 Steer Roping

Most Money Won at a Rodeo

Ty Murray $124,821 at National Finals Rodeo, 1993

Livestock Hall of Fame Honorees

*Bareback **Broncs***
High Tide 1993
Come Apart 1979

Saddle Broncs
Miss Klamath 1998
Descent 1979
Hell's Angel 1979
Five Minutes to Midnight 1979
Midnight.................................1979
Steamboat 1979
Tipperary 1979

Bulls
Crooked Nose (fighting bull) .1990
Red Rock 1990
Old Spec 1979
Oscar.......................................1979
Tornado 1979

Glossary

break (a horse)   quick, dangerous way of taming a horse by riding it until it no longer tries to buck off the rider

bronc, bronco   bucking horse

bull rope   flat, braided rope used in bull riding that goes around a bull's body and is the only handhold a rider is allowed

cattle   cows, bulls, steers, and calves

cloverleaf pattern   four connecting loops that make a shape like a four-leaf clover

flank strap   fleece-lined strip of leather that circles a rodeo bronc's middle behind the rib cage

foal   baby horse

gallop   fastest gait, or movement, of a horse

lasso   long rope with a loop at one end, used to catch calves, steers, or horses; to put a lasso on an animal

mare   female horse

pickup rider   cowboy who helps a contestant off a bucking horse

piggin' string   short, soft length of rope used by a cowboy to tie a calf's legs together in the calf roping event

rigging   narrow strip of leather that encircles a bareback bronc's middle to give the cowboy a handhold

rodeo clowns   athletic performers who protect contestants in rodeos by distracting the animals, and who sometimes entertain the rodeo audience with their clown antics

steer   young adult male cattle that cannot reproduce

Wild West Show   traveling circuses with a western theme that were popular in North America and Europe in the early twentieth century

More Books to Read

Alter, Judith. *The Greatest Show on Dirt*. New York: Franklin Watts, 1996.

Bellville, Cheryl. *Rodeo*. Minneapolis: Lerner Publishing, 1985.

Crum, Robert. *Let's Rodeo!: Young Buckaroos and the World's Wildest Sport*. New York: Simon & Schuster Children's, 1998.

Pinkney, Andrea D. *Bill Pickett: Rodeo-Ridin' Cowboy*. San Diego: Harcourt Brace, 1996.

Index